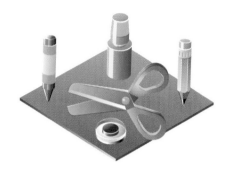

VALENTINE'S
DAY
CRAFTS

by Jean Eick

Library of Congress Cataloging-in-Publication Data
Eick, Jean. 1947-
Valentine's Day Crafts / by Jean Eick.
p. cm.
Includes index.
Summary: Provides instructions for making pipe cleaner hearts,
heart flowers, red hot heart treasures,
Valentine cards, and more.
ISBN 1-56766-537-3 (library bound: alk. Paper)

1. Valentine decorations — Juvenile literature.
2. Handicraft — Juvenile literature.
[1. Valentine decorations. 2. Handicraft.]
I. Title.
TT900.V34E33 1998   98-3248
745.594'1 — dc21   CIP
                                                          AC

GRAPHIC DESIGN & ILLUSTRATION
Robert A. Honey, Seattle

PRODUCTION COORDINATION
James R. Rothaus / James R. Rothaus & Associates

ELECTRONIC PRE-PRESS PRODUCTION
Robert E. Bonaker / Graphic Design & Consulting company

CONTENTS

1 Valentine's Day is a special day when people show how much they care for each other. Some people give candies or flowers to the people they love. Others make homemade gifts to show their feelings. This book will show you how to make some of these fun Valentine's Day crafts. Then you can show how much you care about others, too!

2 Before you start making any craft, be sure to read the directions. Make sure you look at the pictures too, they will help you understand what to do. Go through the list of things you'll need and get everything together. When you're ready, find a good place to work. Now you can begin making your crafts!

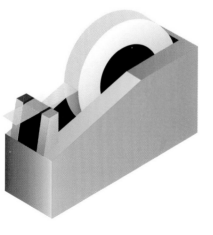

These hearts are quick to make. You can hang single hearts in windows or on doors.

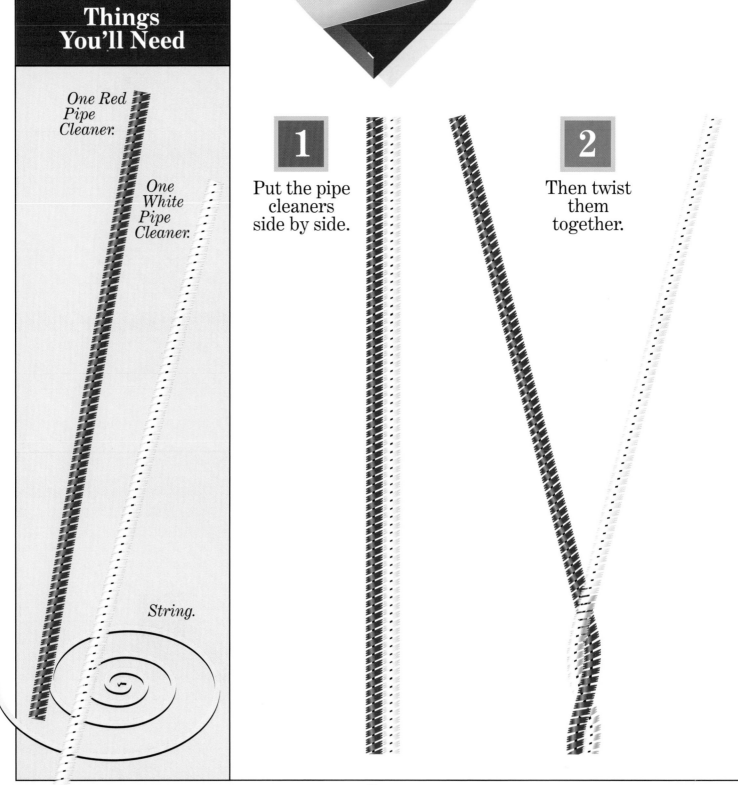

PIPE CLEANER HEARTS

Things You'll Need

One Red Pipe Cleaner.

One White Pipe Cleaner.

String.

1 Put the pipe cleaners side by side.

2 Then twist them together.

3

Do not twist too tight, just firm enough to create a nice and even spiral shape.

4

Bend them into the shape of a heart. Hang them up with a string.

5

You can put them together on a string to go around the room.

You can make lots of hearts in different sizes for decorating walls, doors, and windows.

PAPER HEARTS

Things You'll Need

Scissors.

Construction
Paper.
1 Red.
1 White.
1 Pink.

Glue.   Pencil.

1 Fold a piece of paper in half and draw half of a heart.

2 Carefully cut it out the with scissors.

Things for Decorating

Markers.   Ribbon.   Buttons.   Glitter.   *Stickers Are Great.*

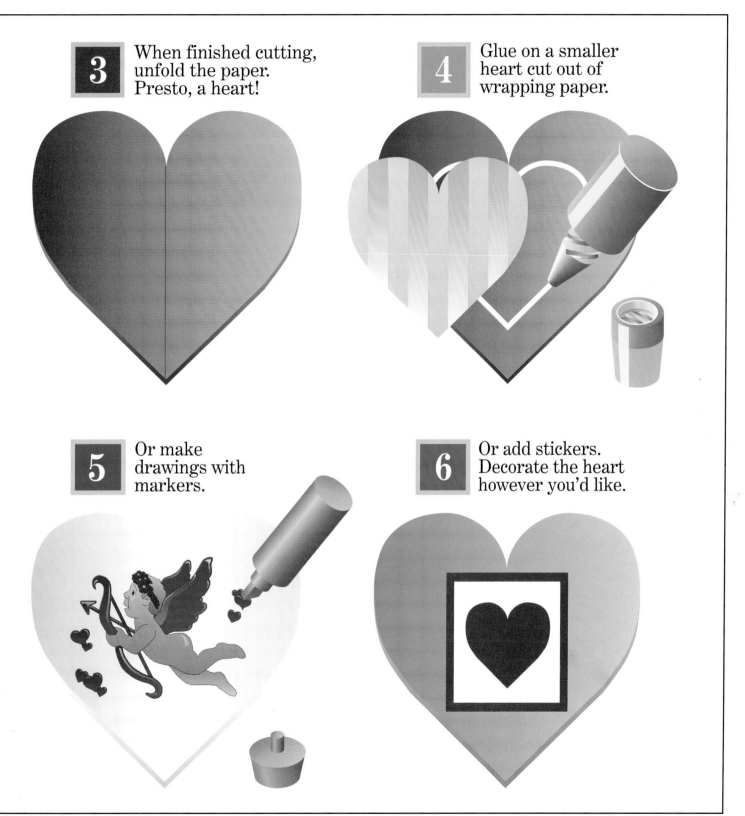

3 When finished cutting, unfold the paper. Presto, a heart!

4 Glue on a smaller heart cut out of wrapping paper.

5 Or make drawings with markers.

6 Or add stickers. Decorate the heart however you'd like.

These gifts are almost as pretty as real flowers.

HEART FLOWERS

1

Make a heart from the plain piece of paper, see page 10 for directions. You will use this heart for tracing other heart shapes.

2

Use the heart to trace 3 more hearts on red construction paper and 3 more on white.

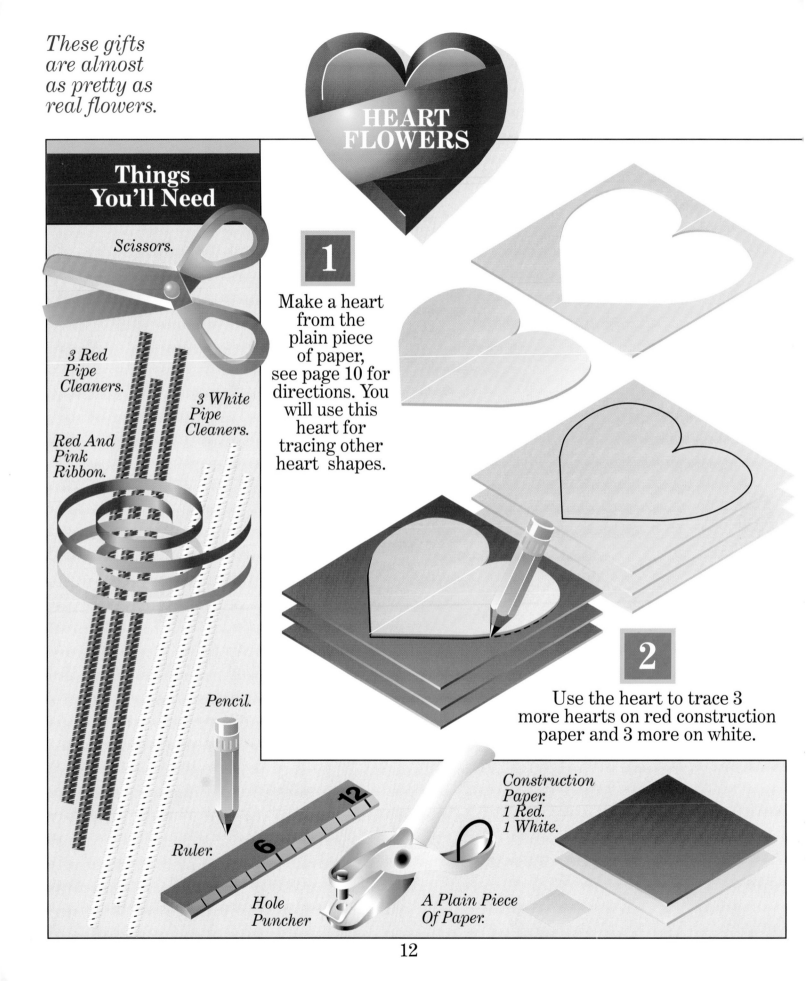

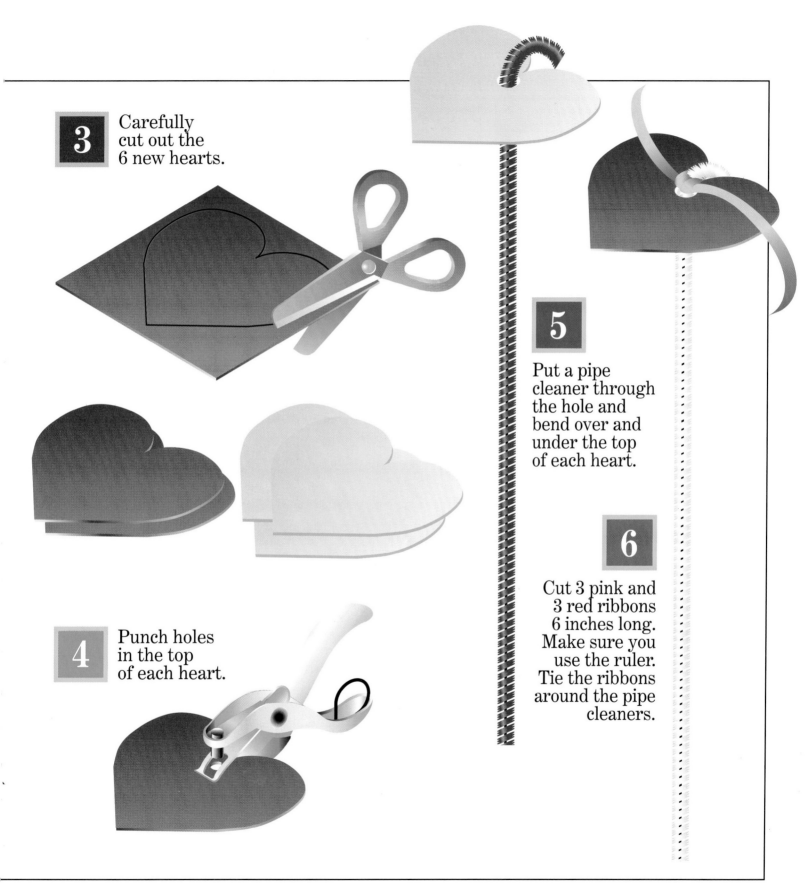

3 Carefully cut out the 6 new hearts.

4 Punch holes in the top of each heart.

5 Put a pipe cleaner through the hole and bend over and under the top of each heart.

6 Cut 3 pink and 3 red ribbons 6 inches long. Make sure you use the ruler. Tie the ribbons around the pipe cleaners.

These tasty presents are as fun to make as they are to eat!

HEART TREASURES

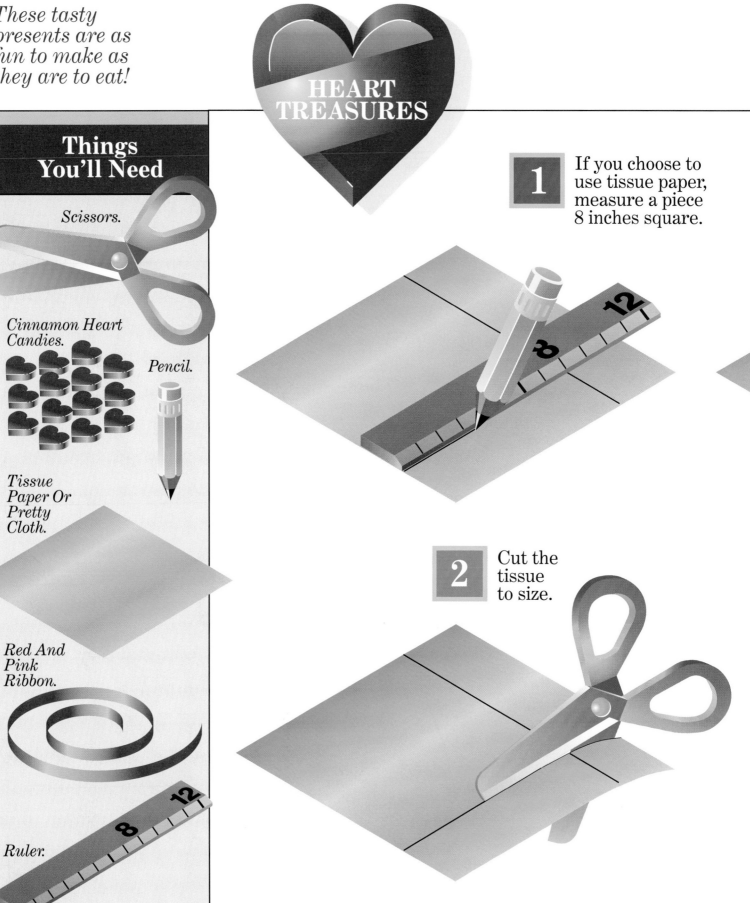

Things You'll Need

Scissors.

Cinnamon Heart Candies.

Pencil.

Tissue Paper Or Pretty Cloth.

Red And Pink Ribbon.

Ruler.

1 If you choose to use tissue paper, measure a piece 8 inches square.

2 Cut the tissue to size.

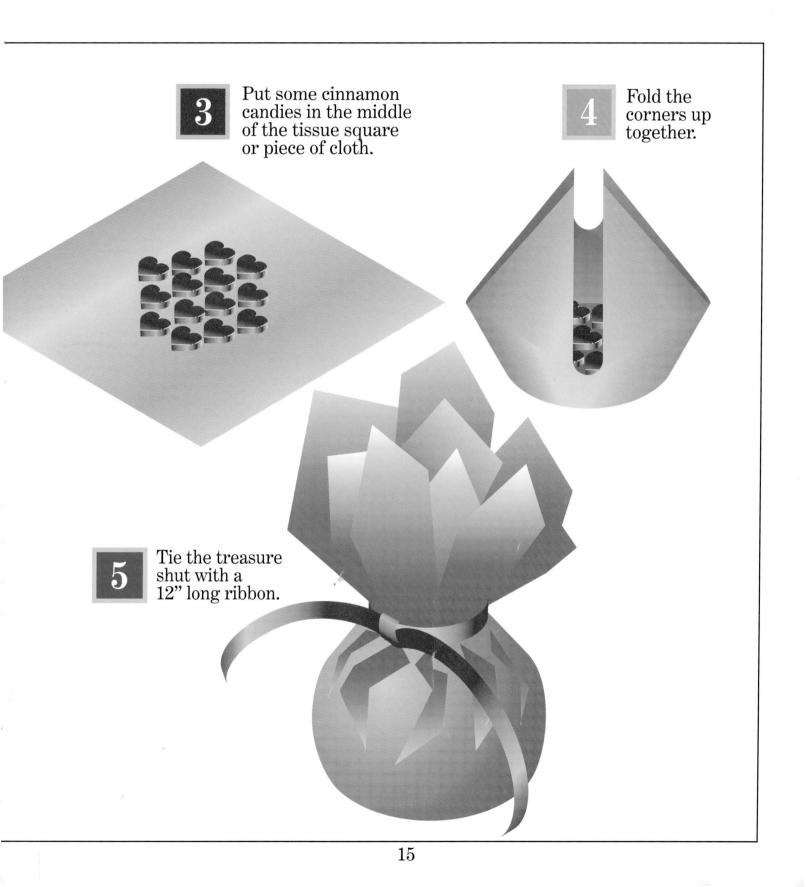

3 Put some cinnamon candies in the middle of the tissue square or piece of cloth.

4 Fold the corners up together.

5 Tie the treasure shut with a 12" long ribbon.

This is so easy to make you can do one for all of your friends.

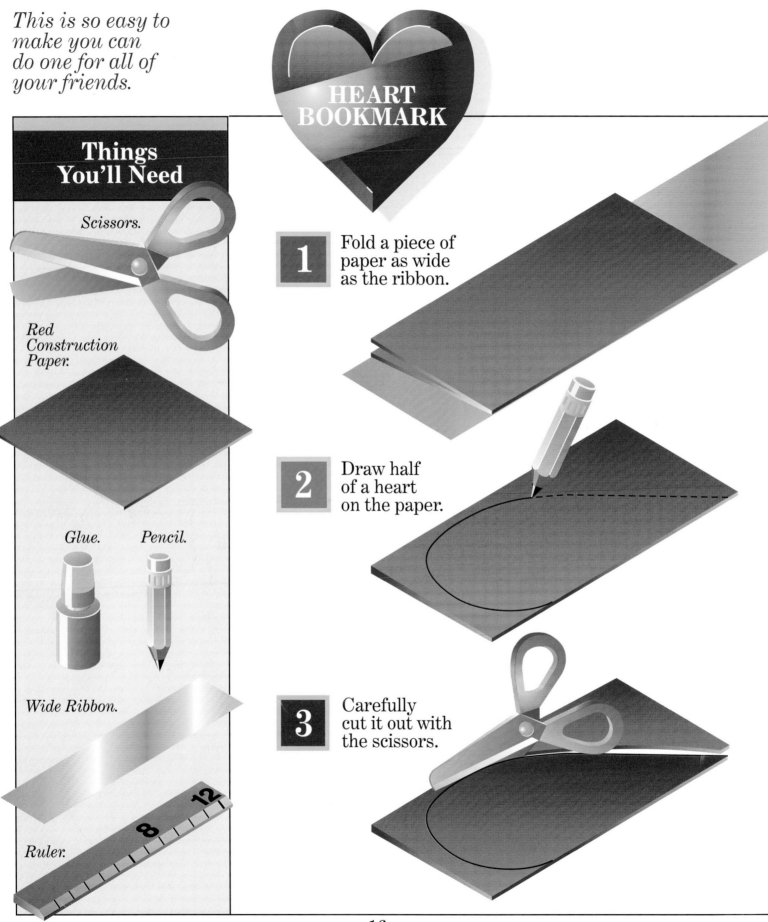

HEART BOOKMARK

Things You'll Need

Scissors.

Red Construction Paper.

Glue.

Pencil.

Wide Ribbon.

Ruler.

1 Fold a piece of paper as wide as the ribbon.

2 Draw half of a heart on the paper.

3 Carefully cut it out with the scissors.

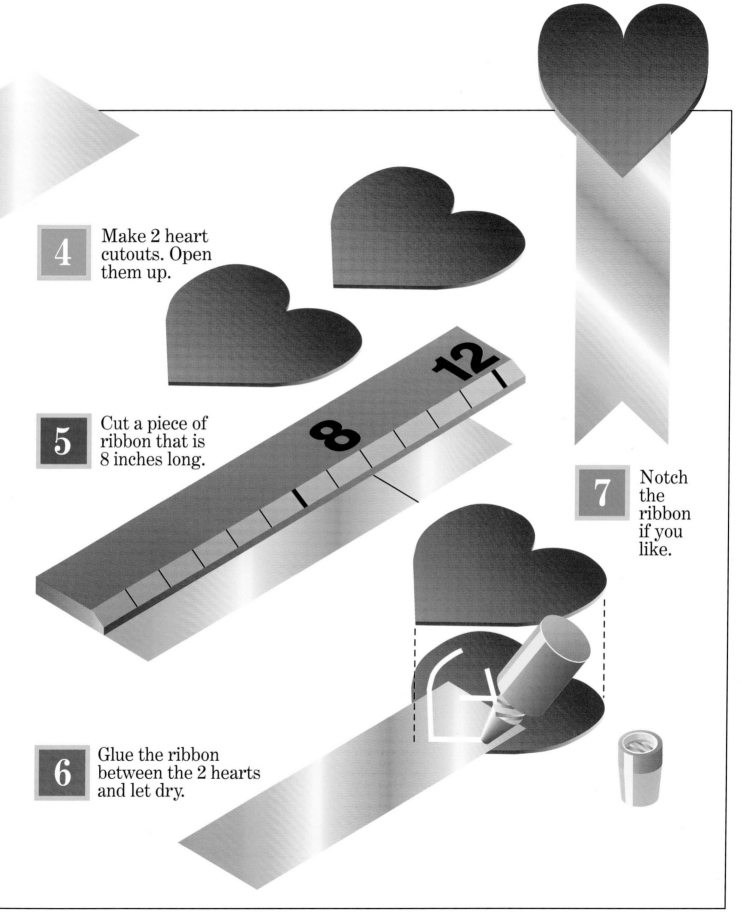

4 Make 2 heart cutouts. Open them up.

5 Cut a piece of ribbon that is 8 inches long.

6 Glue the ribbon between the 2 hearts and let dry.

7 Notch the ribbon if you like.

17

Everyone likes to get Valentine's Day cards. Making them with your friends is fun.

CARDS

Things You'll Need

Scissors.

Crayons, Markers, or Paints. *Pencil.* *Glue.*

Construction Paper.

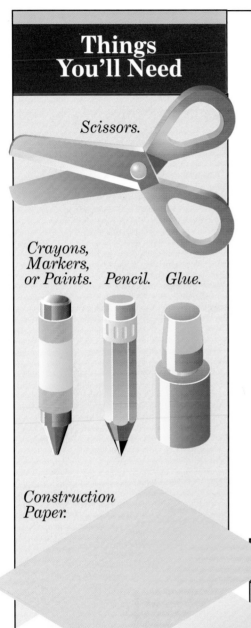

1 Fold the paper to the size you want your card to be. Folding it once will make a large card.

2 Folding it twice will make a small card.

3 Decorate the front of the card.

4 Write a message on the inside of the card. You can decorate the inside, too. Don't forget to sign your name.

Things for Decorating

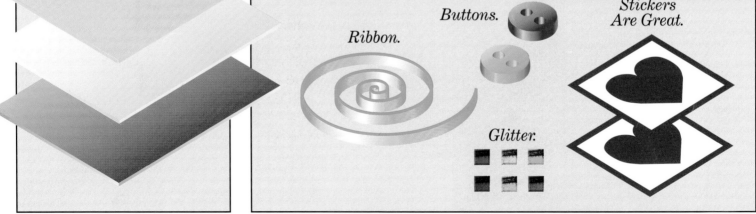

Ribbon.

Buttons.

Stickers Are Great.

Glitter.

Instead of making a square card, make one shaped like a heart!

1 Draw a heart on a folded piece of construction paper. The edge of the heart shape should hang over the fold in the paper.

2 Carefully cut out the shape. Do not cut through the fold.

3 Now open the card. You should see two heart shapes.

4 Take your class photo and a small heart and glue them to the heart card.

PHOTO

? Cut out magazine pictures that remind you of Valentine's Day and glue them to your cards. Things such as flowers and clouds make nice decorations.

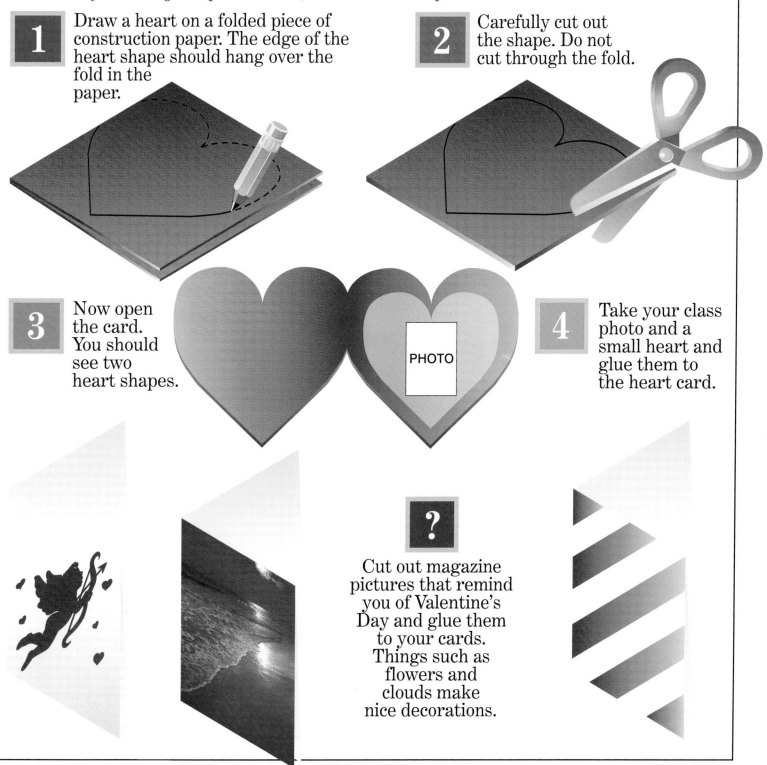

You can even make your own envelopes to fit your cards!

ENVELOPES

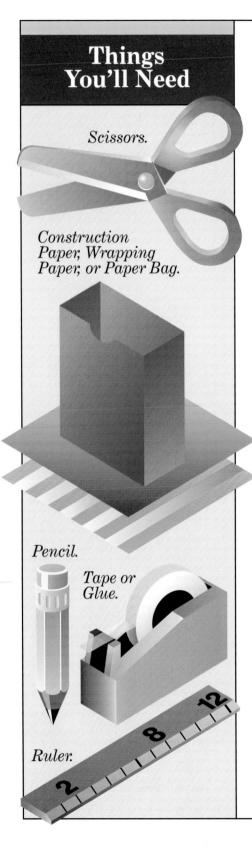

Things You'll Need

Scissors.

Construction Paper; Wrapping Paper, or Paper Bag.

Pencil.

Tape or Glue.

Ruler.

To make a square envelope:

1 Cut out the front of a plain paper bag. It will take an 8 inch square piece of paper to hold a 5¼ inch square card.

2 Cut out a square 8 inches high and 8 inches across. Measure and put an "X" in the center of the square.

3 Fold three of the corners so they cover the "X". Tape or glue the corners so they'll stay in place.

4 Place your card inside, then fold the top down and tape it shut.

TÜRKIYE CUMHURIYETİ POSTALARI

To make an envelope that isn't square:

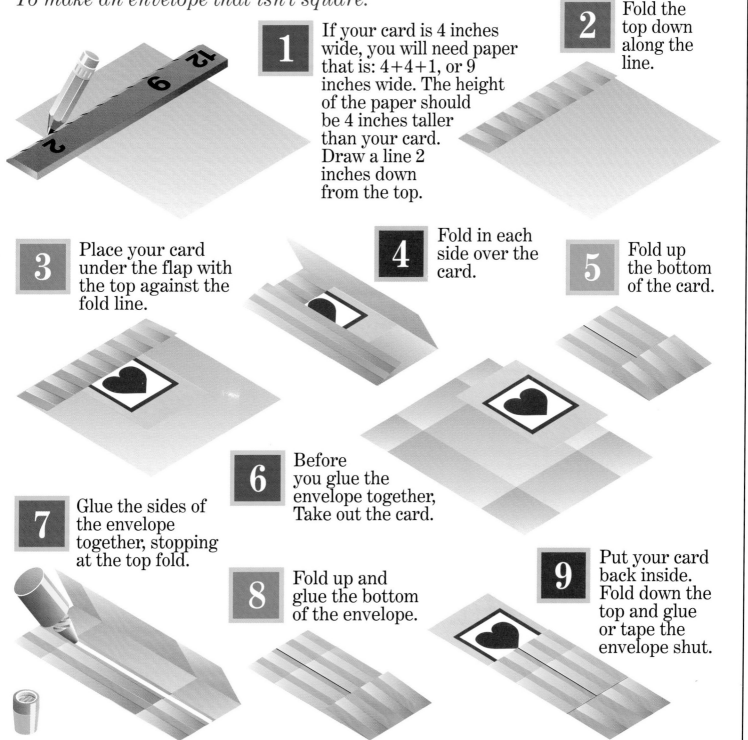

1 If your card is 4 inches wide, you will need paper that is: 4+4+1, or 9 inches wide. The height of the paper should be 4 inches taller than your card. Draw a line 2 inches down from the top.

2 Fold the top down along the line.

3 Place your card under the flap with the top against the fold line.

4 Fold in each side over the card.

5 Fold up the bottom of the card.

6 Before you glue the envelope together, Take out the card.

7 Glue the sides of the envelope together, stopping at the top fold.

8 Fold up and glue the bottom of the envelope.

9 Put your card back inside. Fold down the top and glue or tape the envelope shut.

There are many things you can do with others to celebrate Valentine's Day. Here are some fun ideas.

ACTIVITIES

1 Invite your friends over to make cards for all your classmates. Have each friend bring something for decorating the cards, such as glitter, stickers, or buttons.

2 Have a cookie or cupcake decorating party. Ask each person to bring something for decorating, such as frosting, or candies.

 3 Have a Valentine pizza party. Decorate a room with white paper streamers and some of the decorations in this book. You can play games and make Valentines for each other.

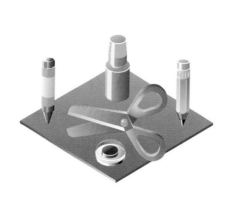